BATMAN

VOLUME 4 **ZERO YEAR – SECRET CITY**

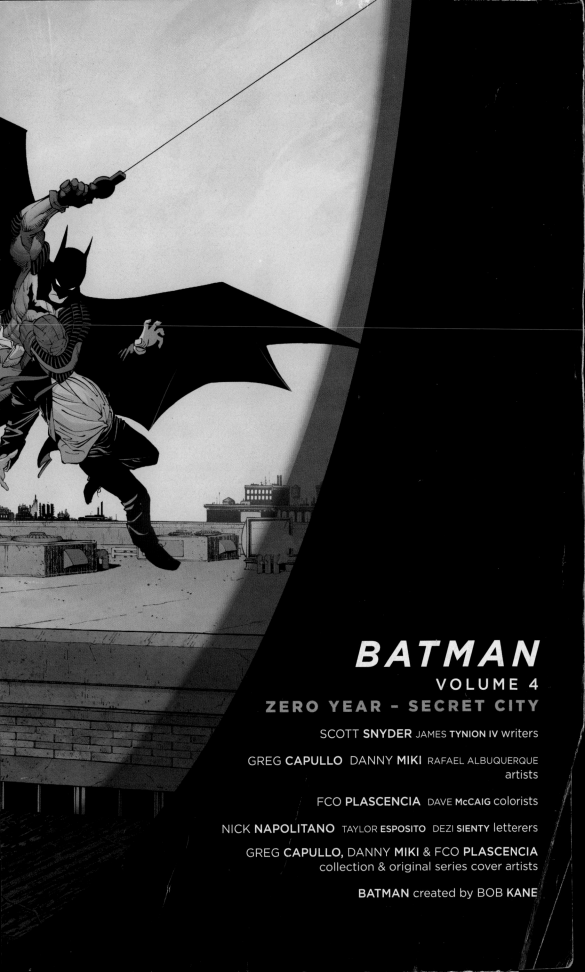

BATMAN
VOLUME 4
ZERO YEAR - SECRET CITY

SCOTT **SNYDER** JAMES **TYNION IV** writers

GREG **CAPULLO** DANNY **MIKI** RAFAEL ALBUQUERQUE
artists

FCO **PLASCENCIA** DAVE **McCAIG** colorists

NICK **NAPOLITANO** TAYLOR **ESPOSITO** DEZI **SIENTY** letterers

GREG **CAPULLO**, DANNY **MIKI** & FCO **PLASCENCIA**
collection & original series cover artists

BATMAN created by BOB **KANE**

MIKE MARTS Editor – Original Series KATIE KUBERT Associate Editor – Original Series PETER HAMBOUSSI Editor
ROBBIN BROSTERMAN Design Director – Books ROBBIE BIEDERMAN Publication Design

BOB HARRAS Senior VP – Editor-in-Chief, DC Comics

DIANE NELSON President DAN DIDIO and JIM LEE Co-Publishers GEOFF JOHNS Chief Creative Officer
AMIT DESAI Senior VP – Marketing and Franchise Management
AMY GENKINS Senior VP – Business and Legal Affairs NAIRI GARDINER Senior VP – Finance
JEFF BOISON VP – Publishing Planning MARK CHIARELLO VP – Art Direction and Design
JOHN CUNNINGHAM VP – Marketing TERRI CUNNINGHAM VP – Editorial Administration
LARRY GANEM VP – Talent Relations and Services ALISON GILL Senior VP – Manufacturing and Operations
HANK KANALZ Senior VP – Vertigo and Integrated Publishing JAY KOGAN VP – Business and Legal Affairs, Publishing
JACK MAHAN VP – Business Affairs, Talent NICK NAPOLITANO VP – Manufacturing Administration SUE POHJA VP – Book Sales
FRED RUIZ VP – Manufacturing Operations COURTNEY SIMMONS Senior VP – Publicity BOB WAYNE Senior VP – Sales

BATMAN VOLUME 4: ZERO YEAR – SECRET CITY

DC Comics, 1700 Broadway, New York, NY 10019
A Warner Bros. Entertainment Company.
Printed by RR Donnelley, Salem, VA, USA. 8/29/14. First Printing.

ISBN: 978-1-4012-4933-5

Library of Congress Cataloging-in-Publication Data

Snyder, Scott, author.
Batman. Volume 4, Zero Year-Secret City / Scott Snyder ; illustrated by Greg Capullo.
pages cm. — (The New 52!)
ISBN 978-1-4012-4933-5
1. Graphic novels. I. Capullo, Greg, illustrator. II. Title. III. Title: Zero Year-Secret City.
PN6728.B36S685 2014
741.5'973—dc23
2014000326

ZERO
YEAR

ZERO
YEAR

Gotham City,
SIX YEARS AGO...

YOU DROPPED YOUR FISH.

...

THANKS.

HE THINKS YOU'RE *DEAD*, YOU KNOW. HE'S BEEN TELLING EVERYONE THAT, EVER SINCE HE KILLED THE CITY.

GOOD. THEN HE WON'T SEE ME COMING.

ZERO YEAR

SECRET CITY: PART ONE

SCOTT SNYDER
WRITER

GREG CAPULLO
PENCILLER

DANNY MIKI – INKER

FCO PLASCENCIA – COLORIST
NICK NAPOLITANO – LETTERER

CAPULLO & PLASCENCIA – COVER

THREE MONTHS EARLIER.

OH, WE'RE *GOING* THERE. YES WE ARE. WE'RE KICKING DOWN THAT DOOR RIGHT NOW.

YOU HEAR ME IN THERE, *AMIGO?*

WE'RE COMING FOR THE MEN IN THE BACK OF THAT TRUCK, AND WE'RE GOING TO *KILL* THEM IN ALL MANNER OF CREATIVITY. AND THEN WE'RE GOING TO DEAL WITH *YOU.*

MASTER BRUCE, PLEASE, IF YOU MAKE A BREAK FOR THE--

NOT NOW.

I ADMIT, YOU'VE PUT UP A GOOD CHASE. THAT FLIP MOVE INTO THE CAB, *WOO!* STEALING OUR TRUCK...

...AND I DON'T KNOW WHERE THE HELL YOU LEARNED TO DRIVE, BUT *KUDOS.*

HOWEVER, YOU'RE AT THE END OF THE ALLEY NOW. AFTER ALL THE WEEKS OF TROUBLE YOU'VE GIVEN US, WE'VE GOT THE CANS TIED ON YOUR TAIL, LITTLE GUY.

BECAUSE THE CITY BELONGS TO THE *RED HOOD.*

DOES IT NOW?

MASTER BRUCE, *DON'T!*

HEH. WELL, LOOK AT THIS GUY.

HE COULD BE ANYONE, ALFRED.

HE *NEVER* TAKES OFF THE HELMET IN FRONT OF THEM. NONE OF THEM KNOW HIS IDENTITY. THAT MUCH I'M SURE OF.

WEIGHTS, SIR?

FIFTY, PLEASE.

NOT ONLY IS HE *FACELESS* TO THE GANG, BUT THEY'RE GENERALLY FACELESS TO *EACH OTHER.*

AND FROM WHAT I CAN TELL, MOST OF THE MEMBERS AREN'T EVEN HARD-ENED *CRIMINALS.* THEY'RE MIDDLE AND UPPER CLASS GOTHAMITES. MEN AND WOMEN THIS MAN HAS STRONG-ARMED OR BLACKMAILED. HE THREATENS THEM, GIVES THEM A A MASK, AND NOW THEY'RE MEMBERS OF THE RED HOOD.

HE MUST HAVE A CORE OF ACTUAL FOLLOWERS. BUT OVERALL, THE GANG IS LIKE A COLLECTION OF SLEEPER AGENTS HE CAN ACTIVATE AT ANYTIME. A WIFE, A HUSBAND... ANYONE MIGHT SECRETLY BE IN THE GANG.

MORE, SIR?

TWO MORE FIFTIES, PLEASE? LET'S GIVE THE ELECTRO-ADHESION BOND A STRESSOR.

BUT IT'S A *NEW* KIND OF CRIME THAT THIS GANG STANDS FOR.

NOTHING LIKE THE STREET CRIME THAT WAS RUNNING RAMPANT WHEN I LEFT THE CITY YEARS AGO.

IT'S LIKE CRIME BENEATH THE SKIN. SOMETHING *VIRAL, HIDDEN* UNTIL IT'S TOO LATE.

NOW, THE MEN THAT THE RED HOOD GANG WERE GOING TO *EXECUTE*--ALL OF THEM WERE LOWER-LEVEL EXECUTIVES, BUSINESSMEN WHO REFUSED TO JOIN.

I MIGHT NOT KNOW HIS *NAME,* BUT I KNOW THE RED HOOD LEADER WELL ENOUGH TO SAY HE WON'T BE DETERRED BY WHAT I DID EARLIER.

I NEED TO WATCH THEM. THEY'LL LEAD ME BACK TO HIM.

JUST ANSWER ME THIS, PLEASE. *TO WHAT END,* MASTER BRUCE?

HOW CAN YOU ASK THAT?

EASILY. YOU DO ALL THIS FOR *WHAT?*

DAMMIT, ALFRED-- SO NO ONE HAS TO GO THROUGH WHAT *I* DID THAT NIGHT, RIGHT THERE IN THAT *ALLEY* OUTSIDE!

THAT'S WHY. THAT'S THE MISSION.

YOU MISUNDERSTAND ME, SIR, THAT'S *NOT* WHAT I MEANT. I WAS REFERRING TO--

LOOK. I HAVE TO GO.

VERY WELL. I'LL GET THE CAR.

ACTUALLY, I'LL DRIVE MYSELF.

LET *ME* GIVE YOU A LIFT, BRUCE.

BUT I **DON'T WANT** IT TO BE, BRUCE. MY SISTER--YOUR MOTHER--SHE KNEW ME WELL ENOUGH TO UNDERSTAND I'D MAKE A TERRIBLE FATHER. BUT I LIKE TO THINK THIS IS HOW I'VE CARED FOR HER, AND FOR **YOU,** IN MY OWN WAY.

IT'S WHY I HAD YOU DECLARED **LEGALLY DEAD,** BRUCE. SO I COULD BUILD SOMETHING NEW OUT OF THIS COMPANY THAT WOULD **LIVE ON.**

BUT THIS CITY HAS ALWAYS HAD A HARD TIME TRUSTING THE KANES. WE'VE HAD MORE THAN OUR SHARE OF SCANDAL AND CONTROVERSY.

YOU WAYNES WERE ALWAYS THE **POPULAR** ONES. IT'S WHY WE WERE ALL SO EXCITED WHEN YOUR FATHER MARRIED MY SISTER. TWO FAMILIES MOVING FORWARD, COMPLETING EACH OTHER. KANE MATERIAL. WAYNE INDUSTRY.

BUT FOR WHATEVER REASON, YOUR PARENTS HAD DIFFERENT, LESS **AMBITIOUS** CALLINGS.

YOU CAN'T UNDERESTIMATE HOW **POWERFUL** A SYMBOL IT WOULD BE TO SEE A WAYNE BACK AT THE TOP OF THIS COMPANY. YOU **CAN'T.**

THAT'S NOT WHY I CAME BACK...

YOU'RE REALLY NOT GOING TO COME INSIDE, ARE YOU?

I GUESS I DID COME TO SHOW YOU A PENNY, THEN.

I OVERSAW THE FORGING MYSELF.

I DON'T KNOW IF YOU KNOW THIS ABOUT ME, BUT I STUDIED TO BE A GEOLOGIST. I WAS ON AN EXPEDITION IN NORTHERN MEXICO WHEN MY FATHER, RODERICK, LEARNED HE WAS DYING.

I WAS, *Heh...* I WAS DOWN IN AN ACTUAL CAVE, BRUCE, FULL OF THE BRIGHTEST SELENITE CRYSTALS, WHEN HE ARRIVED TO TAKE ME HOME.

GOD WE TR

I UNDERSTOOD, THOUGH, BRUCE. YOU SEE, SOME OF US HAVE A RESPONSIBILITY. WE GIVE THINGS UP TO DO WHAT'S SUPPOSED TO BE DONE.

I'M SORRY, UNCLE PHILIP. THAT'S JUST NOT WHAT I'M HERE TO DO. IT'S NOT WHO I AM.

THEN WHO ARE YOU?

BRUCE! BACK FROM THE WILDS.

YOU FIXED THE LINCOLN, DAD?

JUST ABOUT. I'M NOT THE CAR MAN MY FATHER WAS, BUT THIS ONE, IT'S HARD TO STAY AWAY FROM.

GOT A TOUCH OF DEMON TO IT.

IT DOES. YOU WANTED TO SEE ME?

I DID.

WHAT DO YOU LOVE ABOUT GOTHAM, BRUCE?

WHAT DO YOU MEAN?

I'M JUST... I'M JUST *CURIOUS.* I KNOW YOU'RE SNEAKING OFF TO THE CITY AFTER SCHOOL.

...

YOU HAD ME FOLLOWED?

BRUCE, WHEN YOU'RE FROM A FAMILY LIKE OURS, IT ISN'T *SAFE* TO--

THAT'S *WHY*, THOUGH.

THAT'S WHY *WHAT?*

THAT'S WHY I LOVE GOTHAM, DAD. BECAUSE IT'S A PLACE WHERE YOU CAN BE *ANYONE.* WHERE I CAN BE...*NOT* BRUCE WAYNE. I MEAN, NOBODY KNOWS WHO I AM THERE. NOT LIKE SCHOOL. THE CITY LETS ME BE *ANYONE* I WANT.

WELL, WHO DID THE CITY TELL YOU TO BE TODAY?

I DON'T KNOW. NO ONE, REALLY.

Heh. WELL, WHOEVER YOU ARE, BRUCE, KNOW THAT WE'RE *PROUD* OF YOU, YOUR MOM AND I. AND DO ME A FAVOR, WILL YOU? GO EASY ON YOURSELF IN THAT DEPARTMENT. YOU'VE GOT A LOT OF TIME TO FIGURE YOURSELF OUT.

MY GREAT-GRANDFATHER, ALAN, HE USED TO SAY THAT FATE FORMS IN THE DARK. AND SPEAKING OF THE *DARK*, TAKE A LOOK AT THIS.

WHAT IS IT?

A CRAZY IDEA MR. FOX HELPED ME BUILD. IT'S CALLED THE *WITCH'S EYE.* IT SEES THE *FUTURE!*

SHUT UP.

HA! OKAY, IT CAN ONLY SEE THE PRESENT. IT'S ACTUALLY A *VISUAL MAPPER*, SEE? THERE'S A THREE-HUNDRED AND SIXTY DEGREE CAMERA INSIDE.

IT'S DESIGNED FOR FIRST RESPONDERS AT A DISASTER SITE. FIRE-FIGHTERS, EMT'S, OR DOCTORS LIKE ME.

IF A BUILDING HAS COLLAPSED, OR A WHOLE VILLAGE EVEN, YOU ROLL THIS DEVICE IN AND IT MAKES A THREE-DIMENSIONAL MAP FROM INSIDE THE RUBBLE AND PROJECTS IT LIKE A MOVIE.

I THOUGHT WE COULD USE IT TO MAP THE-- *BEEP BEEP*

UGH. THAT'S THE HOSPITAL. I HAVE TO MAKE A CALL, BRUCE. HANG ON.

"HE'S NOT COMING AROUND..."

"...YOU HAVE TO *KILL* YOUR NEPHEW, *BRUCE WAYNE.*"

ZERO YEAR
SECRET CITY: PART TWO

SCOTT SNYDER
WRITER

GREG CAPULLO
PENCILLER

DANNY MIKI
INKER

FCO PLASCENCIA – COLORIST • **NICK NAPOLITANO** – LETTERER

CAPULLO & PLASCENCIA – COVER

AAAH!

WAIT, YOU FORGOT YOUR *CHUTE!*

OH, WELL.

YOU DIDN'T HAVE TO DO *THAT.*

NO, MR. COBBLEPOT. I DID NOT.

LET HIM GO, BOYS.

YOU KNOW, I'VE ALWAYS LOVED BLIMPS. LIKE BIG SILVER *EGGS* ROLLED THROUGH THE SKY.

AND BLIMPS ARE BARELY REGULATED AT ALL IN GOTHAM--AM I RIGHT, MR. COBBLEPOT?

SO THESE EGGS YOU PERSONALLY ROLL IN, WELL, THEY HATCH ALL *SORTS* OF WONDROUS THINGS, DON'T THEY? DRUGS. INFORMATION.

EVEN... *HIGH-TECH WEAPONRY!*

LIKE THE WAYNE SONIC RIFLE! NON-LETHAL →*SIGH*← *BUT!* I HEARD THAT IF YOU REJIGGER THE CONTROLS JUST RIGHT, IT COULD *LIQUEFY* A PERSON'S INSIDES.

OF COURSE, I ASKED YOUR MEN TO REJIGGER ALL THESE EN ROUTE.

WHAT DO YOU THINK, OZZY? TRY THESE OUT AT THE KNIGHTS GAME? MAYBE THE LIBRARY? *SHH.* AND *BOOM!* HA. NOTHING LIKE SIRENS WHERE THEY SHOULDN'T BE ON A SUNNY AFTERNOON, IS THERE?

YAAHHHH--

AAAGH!

WHAT THE--?

IT'S *YOU* IN THERE, ISN'T IT? OUR LITTLE *VIGILANTE!* YOU ARE *GOOD,* MY FRIEND! *HA! HA!*

IS THAT A *FAT SUIT?* AND WHAT ARE YOU, SIX FOOT TWO? HOT DAMN, AND YOU HAD *ME* CONVINCED...HA! FANTASTIC!

ALL RIGHT, ALL RIGHT. YOU KNOW WHAT, SIR? MY FEELINGS ON YOU... DESPITE MY BEST EFFORTS, THEY'VE *CHANGED.* BECAUSE, MUCH AS I HATE TO ADMIT IT...

...I *LIKE* YOU. I THINK YOU'RE A PIECE OF *WORK!*

FUNNY. I THINK YOU'RE A PIECE OF--

HA! SEE, THAT'S WHAT I MEAN.

YOU'RE A MAN ON A *MISSION,* LIKE ME. WE MIGHT JUST BE *TWO OF A KIND,* KID. SO HOW ABOUT IT?

HOW ABOUT YOU COME WORK FOR *ME?* I'M SURE WE COULD FIND YOU A PLACE.

BOSS, HAVE YOU LOST YOUR DAMN--

AAAAGH! IT HURTS!

SEEMS WE HAVE AN OPENING RIGHT *NOW.*

WHAT DO YOU SAY?

I APPRECIATE THE OFFER... BUT I'LL *PASS!*

HMMM. I'M NOT SURE YOU HEARD ME CORRECTLY...

LET'S CLEAN OUT THOSE BIG OL' EARS OF YOURS, SHALL WE?

HOLD HIM STILL.

AAAGH!

THAT'S IT! YOU GOT HIM...

...NOW, LET'S SEE WHO'S *HIDING* IN THERE, SHALL WE?

NO!

UNH!

AW, COME ON! DON'T BE *SHY!*

YOU WANT ME TO THROW YOU A *RED HOOD?*

MAYBE SHOW YOU *MY* FACE? HELL, COME WITH ME INTO THE CONTROL ROOM, I'LL--

THANKS, BUT THAT WON'T BE NECESSARY.

FAACK!

SEEING AS I HAVE YOUR *DNA!*

≈*UNH*≈ STOP HIM!

...THEY'RE STILL GOING.

BUT NO, NOT GOING WELL.

MNNNF!

DID YOU CHECK THE HOLD? COME ON!

HE'S DOWN HERE! I SEE HIM!

DAMMIT!

"WHY ISN'T THIS WORKING?"

...BECAUSE EVERYWHERE I LOOK, IT SEEMS I'M *LOSING THIS WAR*, ALFRED.

COBBLEPOT WAS A DEAD END. THE *DNA* I GOT OFF THE RED HOOD LEADER ISN'T ON RECORD ANYWHERE.

AND NOW HE'S TAKING OVER RIVAL GANGS. WHILE BEFORE HE ONLY TOOK IN NON-CRIMINALS. IT'S LIKE HE EXPANDS THE GANG TO PROVE HE *CAN*.

A BOMB GOES OFF AT A SCHOOL FOR THE DEAF. SOMEONE IS SHOT FOR NO REASON WALKING IN THE PARK. THERE'S NO PATTERN EXCEPT TO MAKE THE CITY AFRAID OF ITSELF.

NO ONE KNOWS WHO TO BE AFRAID OF ANYMORE. THE POLICE ARE DESPERATE AND TAXED, SEARCHING EVERYONE THEY CAN. ALL OF IT BREEDS MORE *FEAR*.

NOW THAT HE'S GOT WAYNE INDUSTRIES WEAPONS IN HIS CACHE, HE CAN SHOW THAT *NOTHING'S* OUT OF REACH.

DAMMIT.

HOOK COME BACK.

ALFRED, IF YOU HAVE SOMETHING TO *SAY*, JUST SAY IT. YOU'RE NEVER THIS QUIET. I CAN PRACTICALLY *FEEL* THE WAVES OF DISDAIN ROLLING OFF OF YOU.

WHAT'S THERE TO *SAY*, SIR? IF YOU CAN'T SEE THE STATE OF THINGS CLEARLY NOW, THERE'S *NO POINT*.

ENLIGHTEN ME.

YOU'RE RIGHT. THIS WAR OF YOURS...IT'S DOOMED. YOU *WILL LOSE*.

I SAID I WAS LOSING. NOT THAT IT WAS *LOST*. I CAN STILL *GET* HIM.

AND IF YOU DO, WHAT THEN? *ANOTHER* LIKE HIM WILL COME.

SO BE IT. THEN I'LL FIGHT THEM, TOO. THE WAR MAY NOT BE WINNABLE, ALFRED, BUT IT'S *MINE*.

AND FRANKLY, I'M GETTING TIRED OF YOUR DAMN SKEPTICISM.

WHNNK

It's not your **WAR** I take issue with, can't you see that? I've fought wars less noble. Believe me. It's **HOW** you're fighting it.

What about it? Spit it out already.

I just **DID.** If only you'd stop and listen, I take issue with--

No, just **SAY** it, Alfred. For once in your life, don't be polite. Just say it, **DAMMIT.**

I take issue with your **COWARDICE,** sir.

My cowardice. **NICE.** I'm out there risking my life to take down a gang that's rotting this city from the inside out. The city my parents loved and fought to protect.

Hook come back.

Fought for in **PUBLIC,** Master Bruce... they meant something. You **STAND** for nothing.

ZZZPT

...You fight as a **GHOST,** and you let Bruce Wayne rot, even as Wayne Enterprises-- your family's legacy to this city--is being run by a sad, angry man with no purpose but **GLORY.**

You refuse to return to your home, thinking it's apart from Gotham, yet the lifeblood of this city runs beneath that house.

I mean, for goodness' sake. "The Red Hood Gang is now using Wayne Industries weapons." If that sentence **ALONE** doesn't open your eyes to your **BLUNDER** here... then I think that your parents...

Well, I think they'd be **ASHAMED.**

IS THAT *RIGHT?!* AND WHAT ABOUT *YOU,* MR. PENNYWORTH?! *HUH?* WHAT EXAMPLE HAVE *YOU* SET?

LIVING IN A MAUSOLEUM, POLISHING SILVER? WHAT GOOD HAVE *YOU* DONE IN THE WORLD? WHO'S THE *REAL* COWARD?

I'M GOING TO GO BACK TO THE MANOR, SIR. THIS WAS A *MISTAKE.* I WISH YOU THE BEST.

COME BACK.

I WAS TALKING TO THE *HOOK.*

RRRGHH!

~SIGH~ CALL PHILIP KANE.

IT'S *ME*, UNCLE PHILIP. BRUCE. I NEED TO TALK TO YOU. IT'S *URGENT.*

HELLO?

KANE, PHILIP

BRUCE, I WAS ABOUT TO SAY THE SAME THING. CAN YOU MEET ME TONIGHT, AT THE MUSEUM? AROUND MIDNIGHT...

"...FOR OLD TIMES' SAKE."

PHILIP?

OVER HERE, BRUCE.

I'M GLAD YOU COULD MEET ME.

I'M AFRAID I HAVE BAD NEWS... A FRIEND OF MINE IN THE COAST GUARD TOLD ME THAT THE RED HOOD GANG HAS STOLEN A CACHE OF WAYNE TECH'S *SONIC WEAPONRY*. AT LEAST TWO CRATES FROM A LOAD THAT WAS APPARENTLY STOLEN BY A *RIVAL* GANG.

I HEARD. WE'RE GOING TO HAVE TO BEEF UP SECURITY.

I'M NOT SURE IT'S JUST A MATTER OF *SECURITY*. THIS GANG, THEY... THEY HAVE PEOPLE ALL OVER.

YOU'RE GOING TO HAVE TO SHUT DOWN OPERATIONS UNTIL YOU FIND WHO'S BEEN TURNED ON THE INSIDE. OR UNTIL SOMEONE *STOPS* THAT GANG.

STOP OPERATIONS... THAT'S NOT POSSIBLE.

THERE ARE KILLERS AND THIEVES RUNNING AROUND WITH WEAPONS WITH THE *WAYNE NAME* ON THEM.

AND WE'LL PUT A STOP TO THAT. BUT...

LOOK, BRUCE. COME BACK TO THE COMPANY. BE A *PART* OF IT. WE CAN TALK ABOUT THIS.

I *CAN'T*.

BRUCE, I'LL ASK ONE LAST TIME. PLEASE--

I'M SORRY, PHILIP. BUT I *CAN'T* HAVE A PUBLIC FACE RIGHT NOW. I CAN'T EXPLAIN. BRUCE WAYNE... HAS TO BE *DEAD*.

IF YOU *INSIST*, BRUCE.

KLIK

PHILIP, WHAT THE HELL ARE YOU *DOING?*

WHEN MY FATHER CAME TO THAT *CAVE* IN MEXICO TO GET ME, BRUCE, I DIDN'T WANT TO GO. WE *FOUGHT.* IN FACT, I SPLIT MY *HEAD* OPEN FIGHTING WITH HIM.

I STILL HAVE THE *METAL PLATE.*

THE POINT IS, HE WAS RIGHT. AND YOU HAVE SOMETHING YOU HAVE TO DO. THIS IS ME, COMING TO YOUR CAVE AND DRAGGING YOU OUT.

BRUCE! THERE YOU ARE!

KLIK KLIK

BRUCE, *VICKI VALE,* GOTHAM GAZETTE! SO FIRST THINGS FIRST! WHY ARE YOU BACK?

BRUCE! YOU CAN'T KEEP RUNNING, BRUCE!

NO WAY OUT THERE, MR. WAYNE.

DO I KNOW YOU?

EDWARD NYGMA. I'M YOUR UNCLE'S ADVISOR.

HAVE YOU EVER SEEN THE REAL ONE?

THE REAL WHAT?

THE SPHYNX, OF COURSE.

ONE TIME, LONG AGO.

SO, THIS WAS YOUR ADVICE REGARDING ME, THEN? THE PARTY?

NO, ACTUALLY. I SUGGESTED...SOMETHING ELSE. BUT YOUR UNCLE DISAGREED.

IF YOU'RE LOOKING FOR THE EXIT, IT'S UP AHEAD, THROUGH THE AVIARY WING.

WHERE ARE YOU GOING, MR. WAYNE?

THE EXIT. YOU SAID EARLIER IT WAS THROUGH THE AVIARY WING UP AHEAD. BUT THERE *IS* NO AVIARY WING.

EGYPTIAN SPHINXES ARE SOME OF THE ONLY SPHINXES WITH NO WINGS. MOST ⇒*UNH*⇐ HAVE WINGS LIKE BIRDS ON THEIR BACKS.

"UP A HEAD..."

TRY *HARDER* NEXT TIME, NYGMA.

⇒*SIGH*⇐ IF ONLY THERE WERE GOING TO BE ONE.

THANK YOU.

ALFRED, ARE YOU THERE?

IT'S WORSE THAN I REALIZED. *MUCH* WORSE.

IF YOU'RE THERE, PLEASE PICK UP. I WAS *WRONG*, ALFRED.

I NEED TO ACT. I NEED TO...DO SOMETHING, TONIGHT.

WE DIDN'T GET TO GO TO THE PARTY, BRUCIE...

"...SO WE THOUGHT WE'D THROW YOU ONE OF OUR *OWN.*"

A SHAME, TOO. YOU GIVE A GOOD TIP.

"IT'S *TOO DARK* TO SEE!

"I CAN'T *FIND* YOU, SON!

"BRUCE, WHERE *ARE* YOU?!"

ZERO YEAR

SECRET CITY: PART THREE

SCOTT SNYDER
WRITER

GREG CAPULLO
PENCILLER

DANNY MIKI
INKER

FCO PLASCENCIA – COLORIST • **NICK NAPOLITANO** – LETTERER

"WHERE ARE YOU?!"

UNH...

"BRUCE, HELP ME *FIND* YOU!"

WHAT DO YOU SEE DOWN THERE? CAN YOU SEE--*WAIT!* I *SEE* YOU! I'M COMING, BRUCE...

...I *HAVE* YOU.

IT MUST HAVE BEEN THE *WORST DAY* OF YOUR LIFE, THE DAY THEY DIED.

WELL, I MEAN, BESIDES *TODAY,* OF COURSE.

I'M SURE THIS'LL SHOCK YOU, BRUCE-- BUT THE TRUTH IS, IT CHANGED *MY LIFE,* TOO--YOUR PARENTS' DEATHS.

CHANGED MY LIFE *FOREVER.*

MARTHA AND THOMAS WAYNE, SCIONS OF THE CITY, DO-GOODERS, TITANS. GUNNED DOWN BY A NOBODY. OVER NOTHING. FOR NO REASON.

I REMEMBER MY FOSTER PARENTS BUYING A LOCK FOR THE DOOR. THE NEXT DAY, OUR NEIGHBORS CAME HOME WITH A SATURDAY NIGHT SPECIAL...

...BECAUSE AT THE END OF DAY, WHAT PEOPLE ARE AFRAID OF IS THE *NOTHING* OF IT, BRUCE. THE *RANDOMNESS.* THE *EMPTY CENTER.*

STARE INTO IT AND TRY TO FIND MEANING. YOU'LL *GO MAD.* ALL YOU CAN DO IS FEAR, AND SURVIVE.

IT'S THE TRUTH.

THAT'S WHAT *THIS GANG* IS--YOU SEE, BRUCE? I CAME UP WITH THE IDEA FOR IT IN THE WAKE OF YOUR PARENTS' DEATH.

IN THAT WONDERFUL MOMENT--THAT TRUE MOMENT, RIGHT AFTER.

SEE? WE WEAR THE RED HOOD TO *COURT* THE WOLF, RATHER THAN HIDE. EAT US, WE SAY. EAT US *ALL.*

NOW, ONCE IN A WHILE, SOMEONE WILL COME ALONG AND BANG THEIR HEAD AGAINST THE FUTILITY OF IT, AND THAT'S ALWAYS EXCITING.

FOR EXAMPLE, THERE'S THIS *ONE MAN* WE'VE BEEN FIGHTING LATELY. A REAL CARD. YOU *REMIND* ME OF HIM A BIT.

IN THE END, THOUGH, WE'LL GET HIM...JUST LIKE WE GOT *YOU.*

"HOLD ON, BRUCE...

"...WE'RE ALMOST THERE."

I WAS *PRESSURING* HIM. HE WOULD HAVE COME AROUND.

WELL, NO, HE WOULDN'T HAVE. HIS PARENTS WERE KILLED IN AN ALLEY WITH A GUN. HE WOULD HAVE COME FOR THE COMPANY. HE WOULD HAVE *TAKEN* IT FROM YOU.

IT'S NOT EVEN FIVE MOVES AWAY. IT'S *TWO* MOVES AWAY. I DID YOU A *FAVOR*.

HERE'S WHAT'S *ONE* MOVE AWAY.

OH, COME ON, PHILIP. YOU DON'T WANT TO DO THIS. I END UP A STAIN ON THE PAVEMENT, PEOPLE COME ASKING *QUESTIONS* ABOUT ME.

AND YOU DON'T WANT IT OUT THERE THAT SOMEONE WITH *MY PAST* WAS WORKING AS *YOUR STRATEGIST*.

WHAT ARE YOU GOING TO DO, DESTROY ALL THE COMPUTERS IN THE OFFICE BEFORE THE POLICE ARRIVE?

WHO SAYS I NEED TO DESTROY THEM? AFTER ALL, YOU ALWAYS WORKED ON A CLOSED LOOP. NOTHING OF YOURS EVER LEFT OUR SERVER. SO REALLY, ALL I'D NEED TO DO IS ERASE THE RECORD OF YOU FROM THIS ROOM.

AND SO IF THERE WERE SOME WAY OF DOING THAT, SAY, MAYBE A POWERFUL *AC MAGNET* BENEATH THE FLOOR, RIGHT HERE, MAYBE ONE THAT COULD BE TURNED ON WITH A *PASSWORD*, A WORD ONLY I KNEW...

...WELL, THEN, IT'D BE PRETTY SIMPLE TO WIPE OUT ALL TRACES OF YOU BEFORE ANY INVESTIGATION EVEN *BEGAN*, WOULDN'T IT?

WELL, TOUCHÉ, PHILIP. BUT STILL, YOU'RE NOT A KILLER.

DON'T TELL ME WHAT I AM! YOU KNOW MY FAMILY? ITS *HISTORY*? YOU KNOW WHAT THINGS WE'VE *DONE* HERE IN GOTHAM? WHAT MAKES YOU THINK *I WON'T*?

ALWAYS SO MANY STEPS AHEAD OF EVERYONE, EDWARD, EH?

SITTING UP HERE IN YOUR LITTLE WEB.

WELL, WHAT DO YOU HAVE TO SAY ABOUT *THIS OUTCOME*? HUH?

JUST ONE THING.

"CAIN."

YOU NEED TO REST, BRUCE. THE BLOWS YOU TOOK TO THE SKULL...AT LEAST WAIT UNTIL THE SWELLING RECEDES AND YOU'RE CLEAR HEADED.

I JUST WANTED TO BE HOME, ALFRED. YOU DIDN'T...YOU DIDN'T HAVE TO *DO* THIS.

YOU KNOW, WHEN IT HAPPENED...WHEN YOUR PARENTS WERE *SHOT,* I REMEMBER BEING AT THE HOSPITAL WHERE THEY WERE TAKEN AFTERWARDS.

I REMEMBER SPEAKING WITH THE DOCTOR. AND HE TOLD ME...HE TOLD ME THAT EVEN IF THEY'D BEEN SHOT IN THE HOSPITAL, IN THE CARDIAC WARD, THE *SEVERITY* OF THE WOUNDS WOULD HAVE BEEN *LETHAL.*

THE THING IS, I WAS ON THE BATTLEFIELD, BRUCE, AND I WAS GOOD. THERE WERE TIMES WHEN I WAS SURE...NO, WHEN *EVERYONE* WAS SURE THAT SOMEONE WAS *DONE FOR* AND...AND I WAS ABLE TO...

...WHAT I'M TRYING TO SAY IS THAT WE MIGHT DISAGREE, WE MIGHT FIGHT. BUT NO MATTER WHAT...NO MATTER *WHAT,* I'LL ALWAYS BE HERE TO PATCH YOU UP.

THAT MUCH I PROMISE.

YES, FATHER.

I SHALL BECOME A BAT.

BUT--

HOOD SIXTY-SEVEN. LISTEN. MY PEOPLE HAVE LIVED HERE EIGHT GENERATIONS. *EIGHT.*

SINCE THIS WHOLE NEIGHBORHOOD WAS DUTCH FARMLAND. SINCE DAMN WOOLLY BLACK SHEEP STOOD WHERE OUR TRUCK IS PARKED.

AND BELIEVE ME, IT'S ALWAYS *SOMETHING* IN GOTHAM. WITCHES. OWLS. *NONE* OF THEM ARE REAL. NEVER WERE...

...NEVER WILL BE.

ESPECIALLY NOT SOME *DEMON MAN* OUT TO FIGHT CRIME.

SO LISTEN TO ME WHEN I TELL YOU THAT ALL THAT'S REAL IS *THIS.* THE RED HOOD GANG. I KNOW...

...BECAUSE I'M *NATIVE ROOTS,* AND I KNOW THIS...PLACE...

...SIXTY-SEVEN? WHERE'D YOU...

...GO?

ZERO YEAR
DARK · CITY

SCOTT SNYDER
WRITER

GREG CAPULLO
PENCILLER

DANNY MIKI - INKER

FCO PLASCENCIA - COLORIST • **NICK NAPOLITANO** - LETTERER
CAPULLO, MIKI & **PLASCENCIA** - COVER

PAGES 44-54
SCOTT SNYDER & JAMES TYNION - STORY
RAFAEL ALBUQUERQUE - ART
DAVE McCAIG - COLORIST • **TAYLOR ESPOSITO** - LETTERER

WHAT DO YOU WANT WITH THIS CITY, BATMAN?!

"...I WOULDN'T GO QUITE *THAT FAR.*"

WATCH YOUR STEP, ALFRED, THE RUNGS ARE SLIPPERY.

SO LONG AS YOU DON'T INSTALL A *FIRE POLE,* I'LL MANAGE, SIR.

THE CAVE ROOF, OVER THERE--IT'S NEARLY AT SURFACE. WITH A LITTLE WORK, WE'LL CREATE AN ENTRANCE FROM INSIDE THE STUDY.

A CAVE HOLE IN THE STUDY. LOVELY. WHAT HAVE YOU FOUND?

HERE. THE RED HOOD GANG HAS BEEN RAIDING BASICALLY EVERY WAYNE DEPOT IN THE CITY. THERE'S BARELY ANYTHING THEY HAVEN'T HIT.

BARELY?

YES. AND THAT'S THE THING. THIS FACILITY HERE...

...IT'S FULL OF MATERIAL YOU'D THINK THE GANG WOULD *WANT,* BUT THEY HAVEN'T TOUCHED IT. IT'S BASICALLY THE ONLY WAYNE SITE LEFT ALONE.

WHY WOULD THEY...

...OH, NO.

...EXCUSE ME, COMMISSIONER LOEB?

I'M BUSY, OFFICER KIVIAT. BY THE WAY, THOUGH--FUN FACT. DID YOU KNOW *BAT SPIT* IS GOOD FOR YOUR HEART? IT'S TRUE.

NO, SIR. I DID NOT. BUT I THOUGHT YOU MIGHT WANT TO KNOW...

...ON THE NEWS. THERE'S SOMEONE CLAIMING TO KNOW SOMETHING ABOUT THE *RED HOOD* GANG.

WOW, SOUNDS FASCINATING. LET ME GUESS, IS THIS SOMEONE *DENT* AGAIN? BECAUSE--

NO, SIR...

...IT'S *BRUCE WAYNE.*

WAYNE? THE MAN'S *DEAD.* HIS CORPSE IS EITHER VERY *RUG-LIKE,* BURIED UNDER TONS OF RUBBLE, OR VERY *SPONGE-LIKE,* LOST TO THE WATERWAYS BELOW. EVEN HIS DOORMAN, *PENNYWHATEVER,* SAID HE WAS--

I KNOW, I KNOW. BUT HE'S ON TELEVISION RIGHT NOW, CLAIMING TO HAVE SOME BOMBSHELL TO REVEAL.

">SIGH< RICH FOLK, ALWAYS CRAVING THE SPOTLIGHT."

"WELL, HE'S GOT IT. IT'S A *ZOO* DOWN THERE. YOU WANT ME TO GET THE CAR?"

"WHAT ARE YOU, *CRAZY?* SEND SOMEONE WHO DESERVES A HEADACHE...

"...SEND *GORDON.*"

"...THE TWENTY-FIVE-YEAR-OLD BILLIONAIRE WAS DECLARED LEGALLY DEAD YEARS AGO, AFTER LEAVING GOTHAM, BUT NOW IT SEEMS..."

"...HE'S ALIVE AND WELL, DESPITE RECENT REPORTS THAT HE'D BEEN KILLED IN AN EXPLOSION IN CRIME ALLEY, WHERE HE'D BEEN SAID TO HAVE TAKEN UP RESIDENCE..."

"...NOW, MR. WAYNE IS BACK, IT SEEMS. THE BIG QUESTION ON EVERYONE'S MIND IS: WHAT DOES HE HAVE TO *SAY?*"

MR. WAYNE!

WHY DID YOU STAY AWAY FROM GOTHAM FOR SO LONG? DID YOU LEAVE A FAMILY BEHIND IN--

IS IT TRUE YOUR PARENTS LEFT YOU IN EXCESS OF--

HELLO.

A LOT OF YOU DON'T KNOW ME.

BUT MY NAME...MY NAME IS *BRUCE WAYNE*, AND I'M HERE TODAY TO ASK YOU SOMETHING. JUST ONE THING. AND IT'S THIS...

...WHAT DO *YOU* LOVE ABOUT GOTHAM CITY?

NO, I MEAN IT. YOU OUT THERE. EVERYONE LOOKING AT THIS BROADCAST. WHAT DO YOU LOVE ABOUT THIS CITY?

I MEAN, IT'S AN *AWFUL* PLACE TO LIVE.

HEH. YOU CAN SAY THAT AGAIN.

RIGHT? I MEAN, IT'S TERRIBLE. IT'S UNAFFORDABLE. DANGEROUS AND FULL OF RAIN. IT'S A MONSTER.

SO *WHY?* WHY DO YOU LOVE IT?

FIFTY-FOUR. YOU HAVE THE BAG WITH THE NIGHT-VISION GOGGLES.

GOT 'M. COMING OUR WAY.

I LOST WAYNE! I CAN'T FIND HIM!

GOT HIM. COME HERE, YOU--

ALL RIGHT, BRUCE, WHERE'D YOU RUN OFF TO?

AH... HE'S THERE, ON THE CATWALK. GET HIM.

AAGH!

WHAT IN...?

COME, MR. WAYNE.

DID YOU SEE *THAT*?! SOMETHING *TOOK* HIM!

BOSS, THERE'S SOMETHING IN HERE WITH US! BOSS!

NOW.

NO...

GET IN THE TRUCKS!

TAKE WHAT YOU CAN! NOW, NOW, *NOW!*

DIDN'T YOU HEAR WHAT I *SAID?* GET IN--

THE BAY DOORS ARE *LOCKED!* THEY'RE NOT RESPONDING!

OH, THEY'RE RESPONDING JUST FINE.

BOOM

CRASH

"...THE WHOLE PLACE IS GOING TO *BLOW!*"

SO LONG, BATS!

LOOKS LIKE WE BOTH LOST THIS ONE! BUT BETTER LUCK NEXT TIME, *EH?*

→Sigh← THAT'S THE IDEA, AT LEAST. STILL, PART OF ME GIVES IT ABOUT A *WEEK* BEFORE THEY FIGURE IT OUT.

YOU'RE SHARING THE JAIL CELL WITH ME, YOU KNOW, WHEN THEY SLAM THE DOOR.

FAIR ENOUGH. SPEAKING OF CLOSING THE DOOR ON MATTERS, I SEE THE POLICE HAVE DISCOVERED THE *IDENTITY* OF THE RED HOOD LEADER.

I'M RELIEVED YOU CAN PUT THAT MATTER TO REST, FINALLY.

UN-FORTUNATELY, IT'S NOT THAT *SIMPLE.*

OH?

"NO BODY WAS RECOVERED FROM THE VAT AT *A.C.E.,* BUT IT SEEMS A COUPLE DEEP MEMBERS OF THE RED HOOD GANG DID HAVE A *SUSPICION* AS TO WHO RED HOOD ONE WAS UNDER THE HELMET.

"THE MAN THEY ALL POINTED TO WAS A *THUG* FROM THE NARROWS. A MAN NAMED *LIAM DISTAL.*"

"AND NOW DISTAL IS STILL OUT THERE, ALBEIT *CRIPPLED* BY HIS FALL INTO--"

"NO. THAT'S THE PROBLEM...

"...LIAM DISTAL'S *BODY* WAS DISCOVERED YESTERDAY. IT WAS STUFFED INTO A BARREL OF LYE OUT BY AMUSEMENT MILE."

"LYE?"

"EXACTLY. THE LYE DISSOLVED THE BETTER PART OF HIS REMAINS. MEANING THERE'S NO WAY TO TELL *WHEN* HE WAS KILLED AND PLACED THERE."

"SO YOU'RE SAYING--"

'M SAYING HAT IT'S ALL MYSTERY, LFRED.

"ALL WE KNOW FOR SURE IS THAT AT SOME POINT IN THE PAST YEAR, *SOMEONE* MURDERED DISTAL, THE *ORIGINAL* RED HOOD LEADER, AND TOOK HIS PLACE.

"WHETHER THAT HAPPENED MONTHS AGO, WEEKS AGO, OR JUST *DAYS* AGO, WE CAN'T BE SURE.

"MEANING, FOR ALL I KNOW, THE MAN I'VE BEEN FACING DOWN THESE PAST FEW WEEKS WAS SWITCHED OUT FOR SOME *PATSY* READING HIS LINES THE DAY OF THE *A.C.E.* CHEM STANDOFF.

"OR, DISTAL COULD HAVE BEEN KILLED *WEEKS* AGO, AND THE MAN I'VE BEEN FACING IS THE SAME ONE WHO FELL INTO THAT VAT AT *A.C.E....* THERE'S NO WAY OF KNOWING.

"HELL, THERE'S EVEN A CHANCE THE MAN I CHASED UP ON TO THE ROOF OF *A.C.E.* SWITCHED PLACES WITH AN IMPOSTER, SOME POOR FALL GUY, WHILE THE *REAL* RED HOOD LEADER, THE ONE WHO KILLED DISTAL, CLIMBED DOWN A FIRE ESCAPE AND FLED."

"NOW YOU'RE JUST PLAYING MULTIPLE CHOICE WITH POSSIBILITIES, SIR."

AND AFTER ALL, WHAT MATTERS IS THAT THE RED HOOD GANG IS *FINISHED.* CORRECT?

SIR?

...

YOU KNOW...

...THINKING ABOUT WHAT YOU SAID EARLIER, ABOUT THE CITIZENS OF THIS CITY FIGURING OUT THE *CONNECTION* BETWEEN BRUCE WAYNE AND BATMAN, I HAVE TO SAY, I'M NOT SO CERTAIN THEY *WILL.*

AND WHY IS THAT?

WELL, WHEN I BEGAN IN *THEATER* AS A YOUNG MAN, I REMEMBER BEING VERY CONCERNED WITH THE VERISIMILITUDE OF EVERY CHARACTER I PLAYED.

WAS I USING THE CORRECT *DIALECT?* WAS MY *COSTUME* ACCURATE? AND I REMEMBER GOING ON STAGE, SO PREOCCUPIED WITH THESE SORTS OF EFFORTS--EFFORTS TO OBSCURE THE FACT THAT IT WAS JUST ME, A YOUNG MAN FROM YORK THEY WERE WATCHING, THAT I KEPT FAILING UP THERE. FAILING MISERABLY, TOO.

"I WAS JUST SO *AFRAID*, BRUCE.

"SO AFRAID OF BEING SEEN THROUGH, OF BEING *CAUGHT*, THAT I MISSED THE *POINT*. I MISSED THE MOST IMPORTANT FACT OF IT ALL, WHICH IS QUITE SIMPLY...

"...THEY *WANT* TO BELIEVE IN YOU UP THERE, BRUCE. THE AUDIENCE WANTS TO *FORGET* WHO'S UNDER THE MASK.

"BUT THEY DON'T WANT TO FORGET BECAUSE OF OBFUSCATION...

"...NO, THEY WANT TO FORGET IT'S YOU BY VIRTUE OF THE *PASSION* OF YOUR PERFORMANCE. THEY WANT TO BE *TRANSPORTED*, BRUCE.

"TRANSPORTED TO A WORLD WHERE BIGGER TRUTHS ARE AT WORK, AND ANYTHING-- *ANYTHING*--CAN HAPPEN. A WORLD WERE THE *IMPOSSIBLE* IS POSSIBLE.

"BATMAN CAN BE SOMETHING LIKE THAT FOR THEM, BRUCE. SOMEONE *TRANSPORTING*.

"SOMEONE WHO *DEFIES* EVERY DAMN RULE OF LOGIC THAT GOVERNS THEIR LIVES."

BATMAN #21 variant cover by Jock

NO! I'VE NEVER BEEN TRAPPED IN MY LIFE! YOU IDIOT SCHOOLBOY! I KNEW I SHOULD HAVE REFUSED YOU! BUT I WAS--

BATMAN #22 variant cover by Mikel Janin

LOCATION UNKNOWN.

AGE TWENTY-ONE...

MY HEAD...

...SERGEI, ARE YOU OUT THERE? I CAN'T SEE A DAMN THING.

WELL, CRAP.

BRUCE WAYNE in
THAT ONE TIME

WRITTEN BY SCOTT SNYDER & JAMES TYNION IV
ART BY RAFAEL ALBUQUERQUE
COLORS BY DAVE McCAIG
LETTERS BY TAYLOR ESPOSITO

BATMAN #23 variant cover by Gary Frank and Brad Anderson

-PANT PANT-

I CAN PRACTICALLY FEEL THE PAIN *RADIATING* FROM YOUR BODY UP HERE.

YOU KNOW THERE'S ONLY ONE WAY TO MAKE THIS STOP.

THIS WAS *NOT* THE LESSON WE DISCUSSED, MY QUEEN.

IT IS THE LESSON YOU NEEDED TO LEARN MOST OF ALL, YOUNG MAN.

CRAK

YOU CAME TO *ME*... TO BE TAUGHT HOW TO USE YOUR BODY, THIS SOFT, *WEAK* THING, TO WAGE WAR.

AND I'VE TAUGHT YOU. BUT TO WAGE WAR WITHOUT *DEATH*... THERE'S SIMPLY NO WAY TO *WIN* WITHOUT IT.

YOU MIGHT WIN *BATTLES*, BUT NOT THE WAR. NO, YOUR OPPONENTS WILL KEEP COMING BACK AGAIN, AND AGAIN, AND AGAIN...

...BECAUSE THEY KNOW YOU'LL NEVER GO ALL THE WAY.

"..." "ALLOW MORE MEN IN."

"I CAN'T, MA'AM. THEY... THEY WON'T GO."

"HE'S...HE'S CRAZY..." "SOME KIND OF DEMON."

"CAN'T FEEL MY--" "GET ME OUT OF HERE...GET ME OUT!"

"WHAT DO YOU MEAN? THEY HAVE TO!"

"I'M SORRY. THEY JUST WON'T."

"THEY'RE SCARED OF HIM, MA'AM."

"THEY'RE AFRAID."

BRUCE WAYNE IN THE PIT

SCOTT SNYDER &
JAMES TYNION IV
WRITERS

RAFAEL ALBUQUERQUE
ARTIST

DAVE McCAIG
COLORIST

DEZI SIENTY
LETTERER

BATMAN #24 variant cover by Guillem March

BATMAN: ISSUE #21
First Draft

Written by Scott Snyder
2013

Hey guys! One note before we start - the feel of this issue (and the next three) should be bold, fun, fast, bright! We want to cut 180 degrees AWAY from the other origin stories. This is where we'll surprise people and make something totally our own - our story is organically brighter and more kinetic and more bombastic, with action, adventure, even touches of sci-fi! So let's celebrate that! Innovative cutting, creative paneling, fast storytelling... I want this to be like an anti-Year One, because it genuinely is, by nature. That story is intimate, grim, gritty, realistic and dark, artistically and storywise - it's a masterpiece, untouchably good, and one of my favorite books ever. But it's mob, crime, grit, blood, corruption...

Our story is big, huge, city-shaking, action, sci-fi at times, adventure! This in no way means it's meant to be less deep or affecting than Year One; on the contrary, I've put more into this story, between folklore about threads of fate, riddles, rebirth and redemption tales than anything we've done. On the surface, though, I want it to feel modern and bright and fast. Bottom line: we're a very, very different beast and we should celebrate that fact in the art, the storytelling, and the tone overall! This is intended as an innovative, bright, and layered Batman origin for today's generation.

Okay - to Gotham!

PAGE 1

I'm thinking we do something here reminiscent of our very first page on BATMAN #1! Three vertical panels, with three views of the city that make the place look almost post-apocalyptic. Should be really shocking. Not so crazy it seems totally irreparable, like buildings fallen down. But...definitely windows shattered, streets flooded, tall weeds and grass and vines grown everywhere, up buildings!

1.
The first, like in BATMAN #1, is WAYNE TOWER, but the glass is shattered. The W broken.

Flocks of birds fly by. Many windows are broken.

2.
CRIME ALLEY, tall, waist-high weeds having grown through the sidewalk.

3.
We're inside a SUBWAY STATION (this one is different, I know) – but it's flooded to the roof with water. FISH swim by. Should seem otherworldly.

4.
Small inset - A SPEAR goes through a FISH in the subway.

PAGES 2-3

1.
A young BOY, maybe 10 years old, African American, in ratty clothes, pulls the fish out of the water with his spear, climbing up the flooded subway steps.

>   BOY: Gotcha.

2.
As he opens a bag of ice for the fish, from the weeds, behind him, two WHITE-STOCKINGED HEADS slowly rise. These belong to two members of a new gang in Gotham. I imagine us seeing them from behind here, looking past them at the BOY, but if you do front, see the next panel for description of the masks!

3.
The BOY spots the 2 GANG MEMBERS, terrified. We see they wear EYELESS white stocking masks , with GIANT MOUTHS painted on the faces, so it's like their whole faces are these hungry, scary mouths.

>   GANG MEMBER: Gotchhhaa...

4.
He starts running! Drops his SPEAR and FISH. They give chase!

5.
CLOSE on a motorcycle wheel cutting through the tall weeds and grasses. (This wheel, of course, belongs to BATMAN'S post-apocalyptic chopper – see next page!)

6.
A BAT-BOLA ties the feet of one of the GANG MEMBERS, tripping him up.

7.
A modernized, cool BILLY CLUB with a BAT SYMBOL on it hits the other GANG MEMBER in the back of the head, knocking him out.

8.
BOY senses a commotion going on behind him.

9.
The BOY turns to see...

PAGE 4

1.
HUGE – BATMAN as we've never seen him before. Militaristic, survivalist, no cape, backpack, straps, gear, a crossbow, rope and grappling hook - badass, like someone living in the wilds.

Greg – of course this design is totally up for grabs! All that matters to me is that it is BADASS and fits the context. We're in a Gotham with no electricity, overgrown and wild. Post-apocalyptic. A dead city. And it has been this way for months. This is the anciently dark, wild, savage, and scary city where BATMAN made his name. A folk-legend... The point is – the description below is just suggestion, brother. If you want a cape, a cloak, whatever, just say and let's talk it out, try it out, brainstorm, and make something cool together!

And he's sitting astride a STEAM-POWERED MOTORCYCLE.

The image should be imposing, intimidating, awe-inspiring. BATMAN – even in ruins, he's saying, this is MY city.

As for the bike, anything you think, Greg, so long as it looks sort of post-apocalyptic.

Or something more train/tank-like:

The key though, is NOT to have the bike overpower BATMAN himself. I really feel like BATMAN in his gear should be the focus. The bike is like an accessory, you know? BATMAN is the star survivalist.

2.
BATMAN hands the boy his fish on the spear, which he dropped.

> BATMAN: You dropped your fish.

3.
The BOY, scared, in awe.

> BOY: Thank...Thank you.

> BOY: He's telling everyone you're dead.

PAGE 4 CONTINUED

4.
BATMAN.

      BATMAN: Good. Then he won't see me coming.

PAGE 5

Guys, I'm thinking of a BACK CARD page, that reads "BATMAN: THE ZERO YEAR" with three, thin, HORIZONTAL SLASH/STRIP BANNER PANELS that are close-ups that don't make sense yet, but will later.

The SUPER-CLOSE, mystery images being:

1.
DETAIL of a RED THREAD going down into the darkness. Greg, we can talk about this - it's the thread the DEVICE BRUCE uses to map the caves is dangling from.

2.
A BONE finger against black brick. [REDACTED] This is just a bone finger, super close.

3.
DETAIL of a LION EYE peering through leaves. This is from the scene when [REDACTED]

PAGE 6

1.
RH LEADER! His shiny red helmet gleaming. Bright, modern, badass! He's pointing a SEMI-AUTOMATIC GUN (UZI maybe?) at US/the camera (and BRUCE) - confrontational- his gang behind him if you can fit them.

[REDACTED]

As for the larger situation itself, we're on the roof of a parking garage in a nice business area of Gotham, right by the water. BRUCE, in escaping the RED HOOD GANG, has driven a TRUCK he stole from them (the truck secretly contains HOSTAGES they were going to murder), up onto the garage roof. It's a fifteen-story building or so.

Facing off with him, the RED HOOD GANG. The LEADER in front, carrying a semi-automatic. Looking badass. There are about 20 of them up here, standing outside cars – nice black cars, like Mercedes, a couple of nice motorcycles. The gang is high-class, is the idea. all in suits like in #0. Those awesome leather masks you designed! And as a reminder, the RED HOOD GANG as an entity is all about terrifyingly random and senseless violence. The leader, RH ONE, he believes that there is no meaning to it all, the plans and designs and lives we make, and he wants people to accept this by joining the gang. The gang is the bloody red truth of things, in his mind, and he is passionate and ruthless. As he represents meaninglessness, so BRUCE will have to combat him by becoming something meaningful, a mad symbol of achievement and the obsessive belief that one person can make a difference.

PAGE 6 CONTINUED

Also, there is a HEAVY-DUTY CRANE on the building just beyond this building – BRUCE is facing it; it's behind the RH GANG, on the next building, closer to the water.

> RH LEADER: Oh we're **going** there.

> RH LEADER: Feel free to take it personally.

2.
BRUCE in the TRUCK, peering out of a fake face. Squinting. The face is tattered and should look weird - a synthetic face like he wore in our #0 issue, but tattered, ripped at the bottom, revealing his own mouth and chin beneath the shredded synthetic skin.

> RH LEADER (OP): We're coming for the men in the back of that truck, amigo, and we're going to kill them in all manner of creativity. And then we're going to deal with you.

> ALFRED (VIA INT.): Master Bruce, please, if you make a break for the—

> BRUCE: Not now.

3.
The SCENE.

> RH LEADER: Now I admit, you've put up a good chase. Frankly, I don't know where the hell you learned to drive like that.

> RH LEADER: But you're at the end of the alley now, nowhere left to run. After all the weeks of trouble, we've got the cans tied on your tail, little guy. The city belongs to the Red Hood.

4.
BRUCE, furious.

> BRUCE: ...

> ALFRED (VIA INT.): Master Bruce, don't!

5.
BRUCE'S foot slams the gas.

6. [if you can fit it comfortably, Greg – if not, kill this panel!]
RH LEADER, truck reflected in his helmet...

> RH LEADER: Well, well.

PAGE 7

1.
The TRUCK barrels forward toward the RH GANG...

> ALFRED (VIA INT.): What...what are you doing?!

> BRUCE: All part of the plan.

PAGE 7 CONTINUED

2.
BRUCE takes a GRAPPLING HOOK CANNON from a BAG OF COOL
GEAR on the passenger seat. I picture this as a kind of mini-bazooka-
looking grappling gun – it's heavy duty!

> ALFRED (VIA INT.): What plan? You can't be serious!

3.
BRUCE puts the base against the wall behind him.

> ALFRED (VIA INT.): But you said yourself, the tensile strength of
> the grappling cable is—

> BRUCE: It'll hold.

4.
POOM! The GUN ANCHORS itself by firing heavy anchoring hooks/bolts
into the wall behind BRUCE – Greg, for this panel I was thinking we
could be with the MEN in the back of the truck, seeing the BOLTS come
through. They're BUSINESSMEN – 6 of them – who are tied up, in their
work clothes, sitting handcuffed, blindfolded (but with their feet free –
they'll need to be able to swim).

5.
BRUCE FIRES the GRAPPLING CANNON HOOK forward, through the
windshield at the CRANE on the next building.

> ALFRED (VIA INT.): Forgive me, sir, but you're not counting the
> weight of six men in the back of the truck! Average weight for a
> grown man is--

> BRUCE: They're underfed!

The RH GANG dives out of the way of the TRUCK! LEADER diving right
by us. As the TRUCK roars off the roof.

> ALFRED (VIA INT.): Your math is wrong! I'm telling you--

> BRUCE: It'll hold!

> ALFRED (VIA INT.): Master Bruce, you're going to--

> BRUCE: Alfred...

6.
The TRUCK roars off the roof!

> BRUCE: ...Would you kindly shut up!

PAGE 8

Greg, however you want to show this awesome moment, SPLASH,
couple panels, go for it - the TRUCK, swinging up B'way towards the
water. BRUCE is hanging on the door of the truck, dangling, as the
truck swings up the street - a truck playing Spider-Man (BRUCE has a
remote in his hand by the way - something really small, so not important to show in any big way)... PEOPLE inside office buildings look and
see this phenomenon. Maybe you can show this from their POV in a
panel?

PAGE 9

1.
When the TRUCK is dangling over the water, at the farthest point of its swing, before it swings back the other way, back toward the garage, dangling BRUCE pushes a button on a remote in his hand...

2.
...Blowing the back open, causing the HOSTAGES to tumble out.

3.
The rope SNAPS, the TRUCK tumbling, with BRUCE.

4.
Everything hits the water!

5.
BRUCE surfaces, the hostages around him, treading water... A POLICE boat is nearby.

6., 7.
The RH LEADER looking at him, saluting.

8.
BRUCE gives him the FINGER – let's bleep this out with a censored panel. Again, guys, we're going for a stylish, wild, cool book! Let's do this!

PAGE 10

Greg, this page is a MONTAGE of YOUNG BRUCE – age 10, days before his PARENTS are killed.

It's just him exploring the city – loving Gotham! Part of this story is about why Bruce loves the city – after all, he grew up across the river. What is it he loves about it? Let's show the childhood joy he found in exploring it. This should be exuberant young BRUCE, thin, inquisitive, eager, a boy with floppy black hair, bright blue eyes...he loves being anonymous in the city, getting to explore without anyone knowing he's BRUCE WAYNE, "prince of Gotham."

As for how he looks, dress-wise, I imagine he's wearing his school uniform, navy blue pants, a white button-down, a jacket with a crest. His tie is way loose, shirt unbuttoned at the collar. And he could be wearing a GOTHAM RAIDERS cap.

Near the top of the page, running across it, I'd love a BANNER, like white lettering that reads: "What do you love about the city, Bruce?" That's the only text on this page! Again, let's be bold, fun!

The images:
1.
BRUCE happily riding the BUS with everyday PEOPLE who don't know who he is.

2.
BRUCE examining a busy fish market in Chinatown, where all sorts of fish are packed in ice.

PAGE 10 CONTINUED...

3.
BRUCE looking up at a beautiful rain of SPARKS falling as a TRAIN passes overhead on the EL.

4.
BRUCE walking across a GOTHAM BRIDGE, taking pictures with an old camera. **And, Greg, if you want to do some kind of cool composition, go for it, maybe a GOTHAM TOKEN at the center of the 4 images?**

PAGE 11

Now we're in the SECRET BASE inside the brownstone in Crime Alley (as seen in #0). BRUCE is at the COMPUTER and on the desk in front of him, it'd be cool if there were a bunch of FAKE FACES (MASKS) on mannequin head stands. Like all the disguises he uses.

BRUCE is hanging upside down, wearing magnetic shoes, attached to a metal scaffolding or bar. He's testing how well they hold him, as he increases the weight. But the idea should be that he's also sort of a resting bat, hanging upside down, becoming...

As for how he looks, I imagine that BRUCE in casual clothes wears mostly black, but he's young, so clothes are rugged – he needs to be active. No suits, no pants and jackets. More like black jeans, cool black sneakers, black T-shirt, and over it, a gray motorcycle jacket with yellow or black detailing (not garish though – he doesn't want to be noticed!) with a black hood he puts up when he leaves. And (also when he leaves) a black GOTHAM RAIDERS baseball cap. This is young, angry, dark BRUCE! No suits, no ties, this is a driven, angry 24-year-old BRUCE. Not wanting to draw attention to himself.

1.
On the computer screen is footage of the RED HOOD LEADER, zoom in so we're close on his helmet.

> BRUCE (OP): He could be anyone, Alfred. Whoever the Red Hood Gang Leader is, he never takes off the helmet in front of them. None of them know his identity. That much I'm sure of.

2.
Big. The scene, BRUCE hanging upside down. Looking bat-like. He's in his jeans, bare-chested.

> BRUCE: Not only is he faceless to the gang, but they're generally faceless to each other.

> ALFRED: Weights, sir?

> BRUCE: Fifty, please.

3.
ALFRED hands him a fifty-pound weight.

> BRUCE: Anonymity. It's the foundation of the gang's success. The six newest members of the gang, inducted last week, all of them were strong-armed in by him.

> BRUCE: Men and women he blackmailed. He must have a core of dedicated followers, but overall, the gang is a phalanx, a collection of agents who can be activated by him at any time.

PAGE 11 CONTINUED

4.
A DETAIL of the MAGNETIC SHOES BRUCE is wearing. The small wires along the sides...they should look like awesome sneakers, with lighted veins of wires.

> BRUCE (OP): A wife, a husband...he gets something on them, gives them a mask, and they're now part of the Red Hood. Two more fifties, please?

5.
ALFRED hands BRUCE another 50 lbs.

> BRUCE: It's impossible to get a read on how many of them there are. Anyone could be a member.

PAGE 12

1.
BRUCE is now holding 200 lbs. upside down. Straining.

> ALFRED: Speaking of anonymity, Master Bruce, forgive me, but isn't it about time you consider letting the city know Bruce Wayne has returned?

> BRUCE: (straining) Unh. To Gotham? I get that you don't approve, Alfred, but Bruce Wayne is legally dead, and that's how he's going to stay.

> ALFRED: Master Bruce--

2.
CLANG. BRUCE drops the weights.

> BRUCE: Alfred, just call me Bruce, will you? Please?

3.
BRUCE flips down.

> ALFRED: I'm afraid I can't do that, sir. When you first asked me to join you in this madness of yours, the truth is, I did so to have your ear. To talk some sense into you.

4.
BRUCE puts some MASKS in a hard black carrying case, like a briefcase, but really hard material.

> BRUCE: I'm more effective in this war against crime like this.

5.
ALFRED.

> ALFRED: It's strange, for years I waited every day for some word of you Master Bruce. Every day, I waited, believing you were still alive. And when you showed up, out of the blue, six weeks ago, I was filled with such...joy.

PAGE 12 CONTINUED

6.
BRUCE, a moment with ALFRED.

> BRUCE: And I want you to know, Alfred, there wasn't a week that went by while I was traveling that I didn't think about writing you. But the truth is, for all I knew, I wouldn't live a month past any letter I sent. And I didn't want to hurt you any worse.

> BRUCE: I can't tell you what it means to have you by my side here. But I'm not bringing Bruce Wayne back to life.

PAGE 13

1.
BRUCE, coming through the entrance from the PRIVATE BASE into the PUBLIC BASE, carrying the case, and also dressed now.

Here's the description from our #0 issue: I imagine it as classy, pre-war, antique but bachelor-ish – a little more antique-ish, library, study, etc., than you'd expect a young man to have, but this is for the contrast with the glassy modern base, cool?

> BRUCE: Now the men the Red Hood Gang were going to execute. All of them were lower-level executives, businessmen who refused to join.

2.
BRUCE moving through the BASE to the door to PUBLIC part of the BROWNSTONE.

> BRUCE: I might not know his name, but I know the man on that screen well enough to say he won't be deterred by what I did earlier.

> BRUCE: I need to watch them, they'll lead me back to him.

3.
We're nearing the door of the PUBLIC BROWNSTONE that leads to the street.

> ALFRED: Just answer me this, please. To what end, Master Bruce?

> BRUCE: How can you ask that?

> ALFRED: Easily. You do all this for what?

4.
BRUCE, turns, angry, but not furious. Not yelling, just frustrated.

> BRUCE: Dammit, Alfred, so no one has to go through what I did that night, right there, in that alley! That's why. That's the mission. How can you even ask that?

PAGE 13 CONTINUED...

5.

ALFRED: I'm sorry, sir, that's not what I meant. I was referring to--

BRUCE: Look. I have to go.

ALFRED: Very well, I'll get the car.

6.
BRUCE puts on a GOTHAM RAIDERS baseball cap at the door.

BRUCE: Actually, I'll drive myself.

PHILIP (OP): Let me give you a lift, BRUCE.

PAGE 14

1.
Large - outside the door is UNCLE PHILIP KANE. Greg, I see him in his late 50s, large in the shoulders, fit. Close-cropped gray hair. I imagine him wearing a nice suit – he's CEO of WAYNE ENT. after all! Let's talk design – love to give him a bit of flair.

Greg, as always, I'm going to leave the composition here up to you – you make conversations exciting somehow, so I'll stay out of your way!

BRUCE: Uncle Philip.

BRUCE: How did you...

2.

PHILIP: Find you? I've had a search on you since the moment you left. In all that time, I only got two sightings of you. Seven years ago, I got a report about someone who looked like you arrested for base jumping at Meru Peak. One more about three years ago. A man resembling you again, for killing a man in Lagos, Nigeria, during a marathon death fight of some kind.

3.

BRUCE: I didn't kill anyone.

PHILIP: Yes, well. All that searching, and deep down I always knew that the way to find you was to follow Mr. Pennyworth. If you were back, he'd come to you.

4.

ALFRED: Forgive me, but you have no business being here, Mr. Kane.

BRUCE: It's all right, Alfred.

PAGE 14 CONTINUED...

5.
A shot as though we're under the lamp where BRUCE'S parents were killed, the BROWNSTONE where PHILIP and BRUCE are standing in the distance.

> PHILIP: God, I haven't been here since the year after it happened. It was right there, too, wasn't it?

> BRUCE: How can I help you, Uncle Philip?

6.
Back with PHILIP and BRUCE.

> PHILIP: Give me a few minutes of your time. Take a quick drive with me.

> BRUCE: Uncle Philip, I--

> PHILIP: Just a few minutes...

PAGE 15

Greg, again, I'm going to largely leave the composition of these pages up to you! For the most part, they're really just talking in front of the PENNY. The one thing is, when PHILIP describes what's happening in the building, the projects being worked on, I'd love insets or small slash panels that show details from the projects he's describing. For example, when he talks about [REDACTED] research, a splash panel of a cyclotron would be great. Like a close-up glimpse.

The CAR is parked outside WAYNE ENT. And in front of WAYNE ENT. is the GIANT PENNY from the cave. It's like a statue erected in front of the building. And the building itself is crowded around by other big skyscrapers, too. So it's like a statue commemorating the financial strength and vibrancy of Gotham.

1.
The CAR in front of the PENNY.

> PHILIP CONT.: "...I want to show you something."

2.
Inside the car. PHILIP is surprised BRUCE doesn't know the building.

> BRUCE: I'm sorry, but I don't understand, Uncle Philip. You brought me here to see a statue?

> PHILIP: ...

> PHILIP: No, the building behind it, Bruce.

3.
The BUILDING. WAYNE ENT. Shiny and new.

> PHILIP (OP): It's the new Wayne Enterprises. I thought you knew.

4.
In the car.

> BRUCE: I've seen pictures. I haven't actually seen the place since coming back.

> PHILIP: We've been doing some incredible work these last few years. We finally merged the families, you know. Kane Chemical is now part of Wayne Industries.

> PHILIP: With our resources pooled, we've become a real giant, Bruce. Not just here in Gotham, but nationally. The research we're doing, from tissue growth to sonic deterrents...we've become a leader in protective technology.

Greg – some INSETS or SPLASH PANELS wherever on the page you think is most striking and is still clear this is in WAYNE ENT.

A.
A CYCLOTRON (we can see it's huge if you put a MAN next to it, what do you think?).

B.
TISSUE DIFFERENTIATION and GROWTH (bone being grown).

5., 6., 7.

> PHILIP: So will you come inside, let me show you around?

> BRUCE: I'm sorry, Uncle Philip.

> PHILIP: You don't approve of what I've done with the company?

> BRUCE: I don't have an opinion.

> PHILIP: You have no opinion. How can you have no--

> BRUCE: I think what you're doing is dangerous, housing R&D in and around the city. I agree with the sentiment there. But you said it yourself, it's your company.

PAGE 16

1.

> PHILIP: But I don't want it to be, Bruce. That's why I brought you here. It's YOUR company. Your mother knew me well enough to understand I'd make a terrible father. But I like to think that this is how I've cared for her, and for you, in my own way. Building up the company.

> PHILIP: It's why I had you declared dead, Bruce. I needed to, in order to take care of what was left. To make it into something that would live on.

2.

PHILIP: Now this city has always had a hard time trusting the Kanes. We've had more than our share of scandal and controversy. This new round of attacks isn't surprising.

PHILIP: Your namesakes, The Waynes, they were the chosen sons and daughters of this city. It's why we were all so excited when your father married my sister. The Waynes and the Kanes, together at last. But for whatever reason, your parents had different, less ambitious callings.

PHILIP: You can't underestimate how powerful a symbol it would be to see a Wayne back at the top of this company. You can't.

3.

BRUCE: That's not why I came back.

PHILIP: You're really not going to come inside, are you?

BRUCE: ...

PHILIP: I guess I did come to show you a penny then.

4., 5.

PHILIP: One hundred percent copper, you know. I oversaw its construction directly.

PHILIP: I don't know if you know this about me, but I studied to be a geologist. I was on an expedition in Cueva de los Cristales in northern Mexico when my father, Roderick, learned he was dying. He flew there, to (heh) to the bald scrub of Mexico to find me and tell me it was time to come home.

PHILIP: You see, some of us have a responsibility, Bruce, a chance to take this city by the horns and shape it. I understood. I took over Kane Chem four months later, and I'm proud of the work we've done there.

PHILIP: Your mother and father, they followed their callings. And certainly, I admired their charitable work, and what your father did every day in the hospital. But they could have done so much more.

6.

PHILIP: And so can you.

BRUCE: I'm sorry, Uncle Philip. That's just not what I'm here to do. It's not who I am.

PHILIP: Then who are you?

PAGE 17

This scene is a FLASHBACK to the day BRUCE fell into the caves. The same day we saw him running around the city on PAGE 10. So he's dressed the same as we saw.

We're in the garage – ROWS of AWESOME VINTAGE CARS – have fun, Greg. Most of the cars are 1920s, 30s, 40s and 50s. Motorcycles, too. This should be any vintage car buff's DREAM garage...amazing, pristine Fords, Rolls-Royces, just beauties, all in a row.

The one THOMAS WAYNE is standing by, which can be pulled out from the line of them if you want, in the center of the room, is a 1939 road-ster. The idea, Greg (and Mike and Katie!) is that [REDACTED]

1.
   BRUCE approaching his father, standing by the LINCOLN.

      BRUCE: You fixed the Lincoln, Dad?

      THOMAS: Just about. I'm not the car man my father was, but this one, it's hard to stay away from.

      BRUCE: It is. You wanted to see me?

2.
      THOMAS: I did. What do you love about Gotham, Bruce?

3.
      BRUCE: What do you mean?

4.
      THOMAS: I'm just...I'm just curious. I know you're sneaking off to the city after school.

5.
      BRUCE ...

      BRUCE: You had me followed?

PAGE 18

1.
      THOMAS: Bruce, when you're from a family like ours, it isn't safe to--

      BRUCE: That's why, though.

      THOMAS: That's why what?

PAGE 18 CONTINUED...

2.

BRUCE: That's why I love Gotham, Dad. Because it's a place where you can be anyone. You can become who you want. Where I can be...not Bruce Wayne. I mean nobody knows who I am there, Dad. Not like school.

THOMAS: And who did Gotham tell you to be?

BRUCE: I don't know...no one, really.

THOMAS: (heh) Well, just know that whoever you are, wandering around the city, you'll still be Bruce Wayne.

3.

THOMAS: And we're a part of the city, too, Bruce. Our family. And the river that feeds the city, it runs right through the caves beneath the house. We're not apart from it, or above it. We're all Gothamites is all.

BRUCE: I guess. Yeah.

THOMAS: Look, go easy on yourself, will you, Bruce? Give your self some room. My great-grandfather, Alan, he used to say that fate forms in the dark. And speaking of the dark....take a look at this.

4.

THOMAS produces a small sphere. It should look like something Mac would make, sleek, black glass, with a laser-camera inside to map things. The idea with this device is that it is lowered into treacherous areas, villages where there've been mudslides, earthquakes, etc., to see if there are people in need of medical help. It holographically maps the area, producing a 3-D replica in perfect hologram when replayed. A long red thread released from its back that you hold onto, as it lowers itself or spins into the collapsed area. Cool? Symbolically, it has a touch of the witch's eye from Oedipus (and the Clash of the Titans). The eye that sees the future, that sees fate...

We're looking at the DEVICE here.

BRUCE: What is it?

THOMAS: A crazy idea Lucius helped me build. It's called the Witch's Eye. It sees the future!

BRUCE: Shut up.

THOMAS: Ha! Okay, it can see the present. It's actually a visual mapper, see? There's a three hundred and sixty degree camera inside.

PAGE 18 CONTINUED...

5.
A laser mapper?

> THOMAS: That's right. It's designed for first responders at a disaster site. Firefighters, EMTs, doctors, like me. If a building has collapsed, or a whole village even, if a town has been swallowed up by a mudslide, and it's not safe to approach, you roll this device in, and it maps the unseen spaces. It can tell responders if anyone is alive inside. It actually creates a three-dimensional map of the affected area that can be played back. Cool, eh?

6.

> BRUCE: Meh. I could build a better one.
>
> THOMAS: I thought we could use it to--
>
> THOMAS: Ugh.
>
> THOMAS: That's the hospital, I have to make a call, Bruce. Hang on.

7.
BRUCE left alone.

PAGE 19

1.
We're back in the present, with BRUCE, sitting in a car of his own, outside the MANOR.

2.
BRUCE, looking at the old abandoned house, the overgrown grounds.

3.
BRUCE looks at the FAKE FACES in his case, the disguises – the idea is a sort of "who are you?" feel.

4.
He closes the case.

5.
And drives off.

> PHILIP CONT.: "He's not coming around..."

PAGE 20

We're now at WAYNE ENT. We're in a top office – this is actually the office of EDWARD NYGMA, the RIDDLER before he's RIDDLER, Greg – though the reader won't realize that it's him until the next page. This page is mostly about showing his office, how odd it is, how smart he is, and what his relationship is to PHILIP. Technically EDWARD is a corporate consultant. A genius strategist, responsible for the rise of multiple companies in the last decade. He's in his late 20s. He looks like classic RIDDLER in terms of hair, face, physique. He's NOT in costume yet. Right now, he wears a green short-sleeve button-down, but all else is relatively normal. He's like a slightly younger version of the EDWARD we know. Before the pomp. He has the same ego, same chip on his shoulder, but not the massive ambition yet. He has a touch of something off, socially. For example, he admits to wearing green because it's known in nature to attract the female eye. He's boastful and annoyingly egotistical, but socially he's an egghead.

As for his office - this is the fun part - at the center is a chair a tiny bit evocative of a question mark, but not too much.

And leading off from the chair's desk (where there are multiple computer screens, too) are dozens, even hundreds of strings of different colors, fanning out across the room, zigzagging, whirling into circular patterns and then straightening out again, a maze of different color strings with each string representing a factor only EDWARD understands – the idea is that this is one big spatial equation – a kind of visual 3-D algorithm for the health and happiness of WAYNE ENT. There should be Post-Its hanging from the strings in various places, sheets of paper marked up, off objects, even, to weigh certain strings down – a snow globe with a Post-It on it labeled "tomorrow's weather." A balloon tied to one string, giving it a bump, with the words "attractiveness of secretaries." Overall, it should look at once brilliant and crazy, all fanning out from the one chair.

On the walls, multiple degrees. EDWARD gets degrees in things for fun, when he feels like it. He has about fifteen is the idea.

1.
WAYNE ENT.

> EDWARD: I figured as much.

> PHILIP: You figured as much. Well, thanks for letting me know.

> EDWARD: I don't understand why you're being so biting, Philip.

2.
PHILIP talking to someone in this crazy office. We can't see who he's speaking with yet.

> PHILIP: It's called sarcasm.

> EDWARD: Precisely, from the Greek, "sarkasmos," meaning, to rip, tear the flesh. Bite. Biting.

PAGE 20 CONTINUED...

3.
We see a stack of framed diplomas gathering dust on the floor. Above them on the wall, A SWORD (not unlike the sword he was holding in Death of the Family - BATMAN #15)

> PHILIP: Well then perhaps I'm being biting because I hired you as my top strategist. And yes, you've helped me take this company to new heights.

> EDWARD: And then some, yes.

4.
PHILIP reaches out to touch a string.

> PHILIP: Fine. But we've stalled is the issue.

> EDWARD: Please don't touch, Philip. That string represents [need something out there] The algorithm is spatial. You breathing on a string like that...disturbs things.

5.
PHILIP, looking angry. A cold anger though. Not explosive.

> PHILIP: You know what disturbs things? A public image problem for one, which we have. The Red Hood Gang exploiting that, stealing from us on both ends, which it's doing. So tell me, with your strings and your strategy, what the hell are we doing next? What's the answer to the mystery?

6.
PHILIP takes the SWORD off the wall.

> PHILIP: I'm getting the feeling you're not listening to me. So allow me to speak loudly by cutting your little cat's cradle to--

PAGE 21

1.
HUGE - Now EDWARD NYGMA – the big reveal. Everything spinning out of him.

> EDWARD: It's not a mystery, Philip. It's a riddle. After all, riddles always seem complicated but have very simple, hidden answers.

2.
EDWARD looking at him over the sword. PHILIP is no longer trying to cut anything down.

> EDWARD: ...and this one has a simple answer, too...

PAGE 22

We end in FB, back in a continuation of the scene we saw on pages 17-18!

1.
Moments after BRUCE'S father leaves, we're with BRUCE alone, carrying the device, walking across the grounds.

　　　EDWARD CONT.: "...you have to kill your nephew, Bruce Wayne."

2.
BRUCE walks across the vast grounds.

3.
BRUCE approaching the old well that looks down into the caves...

4.
Overhead shot of BRUCE peering down into the dark. The cave beckons.

　　　END.